HISTORY OF HOLIDAYS AND FESTIVALS

JUNETEENTH

BY SHASTA CLINCH

Cover image: In Pittsburgh, Pennsylvania, Juneteenth celebrations feature dancers and drumming performances.

Core Library
An Imprint of Abdo Publishing
abdobooks.com

abdobooks.com

Published by Abdo Publishing, a division of ABDO, PO Box 398166, Minneapolis, Minnesota 55439.

Printed in China.
102023
012024

THIS BOOK CONTAINS RECYCLED MATERIALS

Cover Photo: Alexandra Wimley/Pittsburgh Post-Gazette/AP Images
Interior Photos: Carol M. Highsmith/Buyenlarge/Archive Photos/Getty Images, 4–5; Stephanie Keith/Getty Images News/Getty Images, 7; Yong Kim/The Philadelphia Inquirer/AP Images, 9; iStockphoto, 12–13; Red Line Editorial, 15, 25; Adoc-Photos/Corbis Historical/Getty Images, 17; Library of Congress/Donaldson Collection/Michael Ochs Archive/Getty Images, 20; Everett Collection/Shutterstock Images, 22–23, 27, 43; Brandon Bell/Getty Images News/Getty Images, 28; History and Art Collection/Alamy, 32–33, 45; John Tlumacki/Boston Globe/Getty Images, 35; Circa Images/Glasshouse Images/Alamy, 36; Oliver Contreras/SIPA USA/AP Images, 38; Steve Schaefer/Atlanta Journal-Constitution/AP Images, 40

Editor: Laura Stickney
Series Designer: Ryan Gale

Library of Congress Control Number: 2023939653

Publisher's Cataloging-in-Publication Data
Names: Clinch, Shasta, author.
Title: Juneteenth / by Shasta Clinch
Description: Minneapolis, Minnesota: Abdo Publishing, 2024 | Series: History of holidays and festivals | Includes online resources and index.
Identifiers: ISBN 9781098292621 (lib. bdg.) | ISBN 9798384910565 (ebook)
Subjects: LCSH: Holidays--Juvenile literature. | Festivals--Juvenile literature. | Juneteenth--Juvenile literature. | Black Independence Day--Juvenile literature. | African Americans--Social life and customs--Juvenile literature. | Slaves--Emancipation--Juvenile literature.
Classification: DDC 394.263--dc23

CONTENTS

CHAPTER ONE

ONE DAY IN TEXAS

Sierra woke up early. She ran to her little brother Karl's bedroom to wake him up. Sierra was excited because it was Juneteenth. Every year on June 19, her family celebrated the anniversary of when enslaved people in Texas learned that they had been freed. Growing up in Galveston, Texas, Sierra had been celebrating Juneteenth her whole life. But this year, 2021, felt different. It was the first time Juneteenth didn't feel like a holiday that only people in Galveston celebrate.

Some people believe General Order No. 3 was read aloud from the balcony or grounds of Ashton Villa. Every year, people gather at the villa to listen to reenactors read the order.

It had been declared a federal holiday. This means it is officially recognized by the US government.

As Sierra raised her hand to knock on her brother's door, it opened quickly. Karl was already up! The two ran downstairs to have breakfast with their parents. Then they made their way to downtown Galveston to participate in the Juneteenth Freedom Walk. During the walk, they made five stops at important locations in Galveston. These places honor the history of enslaved people in the United States. The first stop was Pier 21, where many Black people arrived in Texas. Stop two was a former army headquarters where General Order No. 3 was written. This document informed people in Texas that all enslaved people were free.

The third stop was the US Customs House, where copies of the order were printed. The next location, Reedy Chapel A.M.E. Church, was formerly known as the Negro Church on Broadway. Here, a copy of the order had been posted. It was one of the only places Black people could gather at the time. The last stop

Many US cities hold outdoor Juneteenth events at local parks. People gather to enjoy music, games, food, and other activities.

was Ashton Villa, where many believe General Order No. 3 was read aloud. Sierra and her family listened to a reenactor read the order. Every time Sierra heard the words "all slaves are free," she got excited. She imagined the joy that formerly enslaved people must have felt when they heard those words.

The rest of Sierra's day would be spent at a parade and then a big barbecue at a local park. For Sierra, her family, and Black people all over the United States, Juneteenth is a special day to celebrate their history and culture. It is a time for everyone to learn more about slavery in the United States and the bravery

PERSPECTIVES

SLAVE VS. ENSLAVED

Slavery in the United States was based on the idea that Black people were less than human. Some historians believe that using the word *slave* continues this idea because it defines a person by their status as property. It is a noun that defines the person's identity. Instead, these historians recommend using *enslaved person*. This term describes someone who was forced into slavery. The historians argue that using *enslaved person* is a conscious way of talking about a person by affirming his or her humanity. It recognizes that the person was placed in this circumstance by another person.

of the people who fought to end it. It is an opportunity for people of different backgrounds to share in the joy of being free.

WHAT IS JUNETEENTH?

Juneteenth is a holiday observed every year on June 19. Juneteenth is a combination of the words "June" and "nineteenth." It has also been called Juneteenth Independence Day, Freedom Day, and Emancipation Day.

In some modern Juneteenth celebrations, people dress in historical uniforms to honor Black soldiers who fought in the Civil War.

It is a day that celebrates the emancipation of enslaved people in the United States. Emancipation means being set free.

In the United States, Black people were enslaved for hundreds of years. Enslaved people were seen as the property of others. They were considered less than people. They could not own property or vote. And they were forced to do brutal work for no pay. In January 1863, President Abraham Lincoln signed the Emancipation Proclamation. This document declared that enslaved people living in the South were now free. At the time, the Northern and Southern states were

MORE THAN THE DOCUMENTS

General Order No. 3 and the Emancipation Proclamation are important historical documents that played a role in ending slavery. But many Black people also worked hard to end the practice. Many fought to free themselves. Nat Turner, for example, was an enslaved man who led a major rebellion in Virginia in 1831. Harriet Tubman escaped slavery and helped other enslaved people escape by guiding them to the North. Frederick Douglass spent his life advocating for abolishing, or ending, slavery. Turner, Tubman, Douglass, and many other Black people all contributed to this turning point in US history.

fighting each other in the American Civil War (1861–1865). They were fighting over the issue of slavery. The Northern states, which were against slavery, were called the Union. The Southern states that wanted to keep slavery were called the Confederate States of America, or the Confederacy.

Texas was the westernmost Confederate state during the war. News took a longer time to reach Texas.

There were no phones or internet at the time. Because of this, it was easier for white enslavers in Texas to keep the news of freedom from Black people. As the Civil War raged on, many enslavers left other Southern states. They went to Texas, where Union soldiers had not yet arrived. This meant many Black people in the South did not yet know that they had been freed.

On June 19, 1865, enslaved Black people in Texas heard for the first time that they would no longer be the property of others. Many people recognize this day as the end of slavery. One year later, in 1866, the first Juneteenth celebration took place.

EXPLORE ONLINE

Chapter One discusses the history of Juneteenth and modern Juneteenth celebrations. The video at the website below goes into more depth on this topic. What new information did you learn from the video?

JUNETEENTH

abdocorelibrary.com/juneteenth

SALE
BY

CHAPTER TWO

THE HISTORY OF SLAVERY

Slavery has existed around the world for thousands of years. The transatlantic slave trade started in the late 1400s and early 1500s, when European people began venturing into Africa. The Europeans enslaved African people and sent them to the Americas. This slave trade marked the beginning of slavery based on race. Many Europeans justified this practice by saying that Black people were inferior to or not as valuable as white people.

The slave trade separated many families. Enslaved people were often sold away from their children, parents, siblings, and spouses.

THE TRANSATLANTIC SLAVE TRADE

Through the transatlantic slave trade, about 12.5 million people were taken from Africa and sold into slavery around the world. This was part of a global trade system. Goods such as cloth, guns, and alcohol were taken to Africa and traded for enslaved Africans.

Sometimes African men, women, and children were captured by their neighbors, who traded them to Europeans. But later, Europeans began to capture people themselves. These captives were taken to the Americas. Many were forced to work on large farms called plantations. Plantations produced raw goods such as sugar, coffee, cotton, and tobacco. These goods were sold in Europe and used to make other products.

The people kidnapped from Africa were forced onto ships and taken across the Atlantic Ocean. Inside the ships, they were chained together in the lower decks. Often, there wasn't enough room for people to sit up. Conditions on the ships were so bad that nearly 25 percent of enslaved people died before reaching

THE TRANSATLANTIC
SLAVE TRADE

This map shows the global triangular trade system. How do you think this trade system started? What impacts do you think it had on each continent?

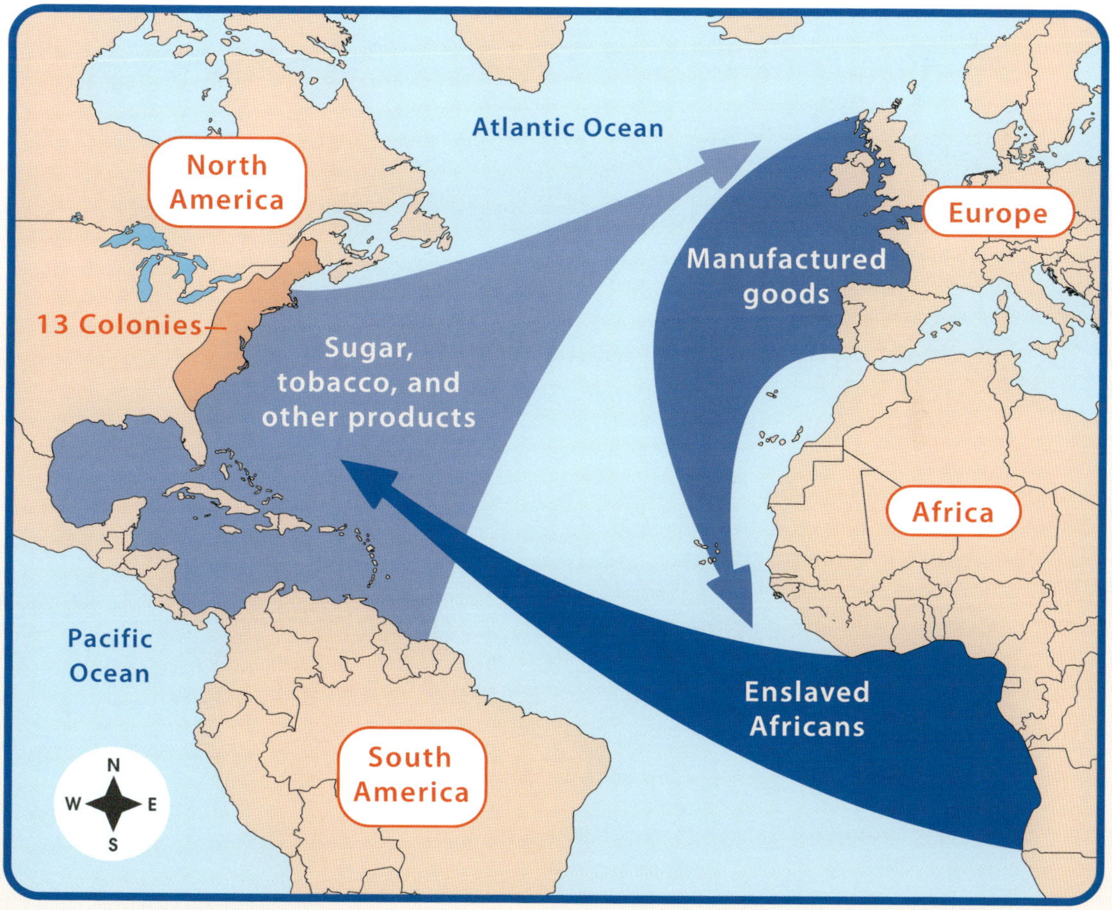

their destinations. But the slave trade continued for centuries. It made many people very rich and powerful.

SLAVERY IN THE UNITED STATES

Before the United States became a country, people from England set up colonies in North America. These became the 13 US colonies. The first enslaved people in the colonies arrived in 1619. They were captured from West Africa and brought to Jamestown, Virginia, to work in tobacco fields. These enslaved people helped make Virginia the largest and richest US colony.

Slavery in the United States was brutal. Once a person was enslaved, he or she remained enslaved forever. A 1662 law said babies born to enslaved people became enslaved too. Some enslaved people worked all day in fields, picking cotton, planting tobacco, or harvesting indigo. They had to work with little food and in scorching heat. Other enslaved people worked in enslavers' houses, doing housework or caring for children. If enslaved people resisted, they were often

On many plantations, enslaved men, women, and children were all forced to work long hours in fields. Their tasks included planting, hoeing, and harvesting crops.

severely punished or beaten. Sometimes they were sold and separated from their families.

Enslaved people made many contributions to the United States. They cleared land and constructed buildings. Enslaved people helped build the White House and the plantations of leaders such as George Washington and Thomas Jefferson. In the Revolutionary War (1775–1783), the 13 colonies won independence from England. They became the United States. But the war was expensive. The United States had borrowed money from other countries to pay for everything the army needed to fight. Money made from enslaved

RELIGION ON PLANTATIONS

Religion played a big role in many enslaved people's lives. They had brought their religious practices with them from West Africa. Some enslaved people attended churches alongside white people, including enslavers. Others founded their own churches. Some enslavers forbade Black people from attending services. But enslaved people still found ways to worship. They kept their faith alive through secret gatherings, dances, and folktales. Many made up spirituals, or songs with Christian themes, that talked about freedom. One example is the song "Swing Low, Sweet Chariot." Many spirituals featured a story from the Christian Bible about God leading enslaved people out of Egypt.

people's work helped the country pay off these debts.

AFTER THE REVOLUTION

In 1776, representatives of the 13 colonies signed the Declaration of Independence. This document officially announced that the colonies were no longer part of Great Britain. The declaration said that all men are created equal. But when it was written, no Black people in the country were considered equal to the signers of the declaration, who were all white men.

While slavery continued in the country after the war, some people in the North began speaking out against it. These people were known as abolitionists. They believed slavery was wrong. They worked to end the practice by urging the US Congress to change laws. They published antislavery books and newspapers. They made speeches

PERSPECTIVES

THE UNDERGROUND RAILROAD

Some abolitionists worked to free enslaved people. In the early 1800s, they established the Underground Railroad. This secret system of safe locations helped enslaved people from the South seek freedom in the North. Harriet Tubman escaped from slavery in 1849. After escaping, she returned to the Underground Railroad 13 times and helped free about 70 people. In 1896, Tubman said, "I was the conductor of the Underground Railroad for eight years, and I can say what most conductors can't say—I never ran my train off the track and I never lost a passenger."

Some abolitionists were people who had escaped slavery, such as Harriet Tubman. Tubman escaped when she was 27 years old. She went on to rescue other enslaved people and work as a spy for the Union during the Civil War.

and ran for political office. By 1804, all Northern states had ended the practice of slavery or started the process of abolishing it. In 1808, it became illegal to bring in enslaved people from outside the United States. But slavery remained a big part of the economy in the South. Slavery made some white people in the South rich and powerful. Because of this, they wanted the practice to continue. Disagreements about slavery caused tensions to rise between the Northern and Southern states.

STRAIGHT TO THE SOURCE

Frederick Douglass escaped slavery in 1838. In 1852, the Rochester Ladies' Anti-Slavery Sewing Society invited Douglass to give a speech celebrating the Fourth of July. In it, he said the following:

> *What have I, or those I represent, to do with your national independence? Are the great principles of political freedom and of natural justice, embodied in that Declaration of Independence, extended to us? . . . I say it with a sad sense of the disparity between us. I am not included within the pale of glorious anniversary! Your high independence only reveals the immeasurable distance between us. The blessings in which you, this day, rejoice, are not enjoyed in common. The rich inheritance of justice, liberty, prosperity, and independence, bequeathed by your fathers, is shared by you, not by me. . . . This Fourth July is yours, not mine. You may rejoice, I must mourn.*

Source: "A Nation's Story." *National Museum of African American History and Culture*, n.d., nmaahc.si.edu. Accessed 28 Apr. 2023.

WHAT'S THE BIG IDEA?

Take a close look at this excerpt. What is Douglass's main point? What does he say about the Fourth of July? Write down two or three pieces of evidence Douglass uses to make the point.

54TH MASS

CHAPTER THREE

THE CIVIL WAR

By the 1850s, slavery was dividing the United States. In the North, abolitionists called for the end of the practice. In the South, politicians and people connected to the agriculture industry wanted slavery to stay. In November 1860, Abraham Lincoln was elected president. He was not popular in the South because he opposed slavery. People in the South feared that Lincoln would abolish slavery. So several southern states seceded, or separated, from the Union. In December

By the end of the Civil War, around 180,000 Black soldiers had joined the Union army. One well-known group of Black soldiers was the 54th Massachusetts Volunteer Infantry Regiment.

1860, South Carolina became the first state to secede. By February 1861, Mississippi, Florida, Alabama, Georgia, Louisiana, and Texas had also seceded. These states established the Confederate States of America. Jefferson Davis became their president.

The Confederate States wrote their own constitution. Confederate vice president Alexander Stephens gave a speech introducing it. He declared that the country and its government was founded "upon the great truth that the negro is not equal to the white man." This speech became known as the Cornerstone Speech. A few weeks later, the Civil War started. By April 15, Virginia, North Carolina, Tennessee, and Arkansas had also joined the Confederacy.

THE EMANCIPATION PROCLAMATION

On January 1, 1863, Abraham Lincoln signed the Emancipation Proclamation. It said all enslaved people in the states that were rebelling against the Union "shall be then, thenceforward, and forever free."

THE WAR BETWEEN THE STATES

This map shows which states were part of the Union and which states were part of the Confederacy during the Civil War. It also shows the border states, which supported the Union but still allowed slavery. The Union controlled most of the US territories. What do you notice about the divide between the states?

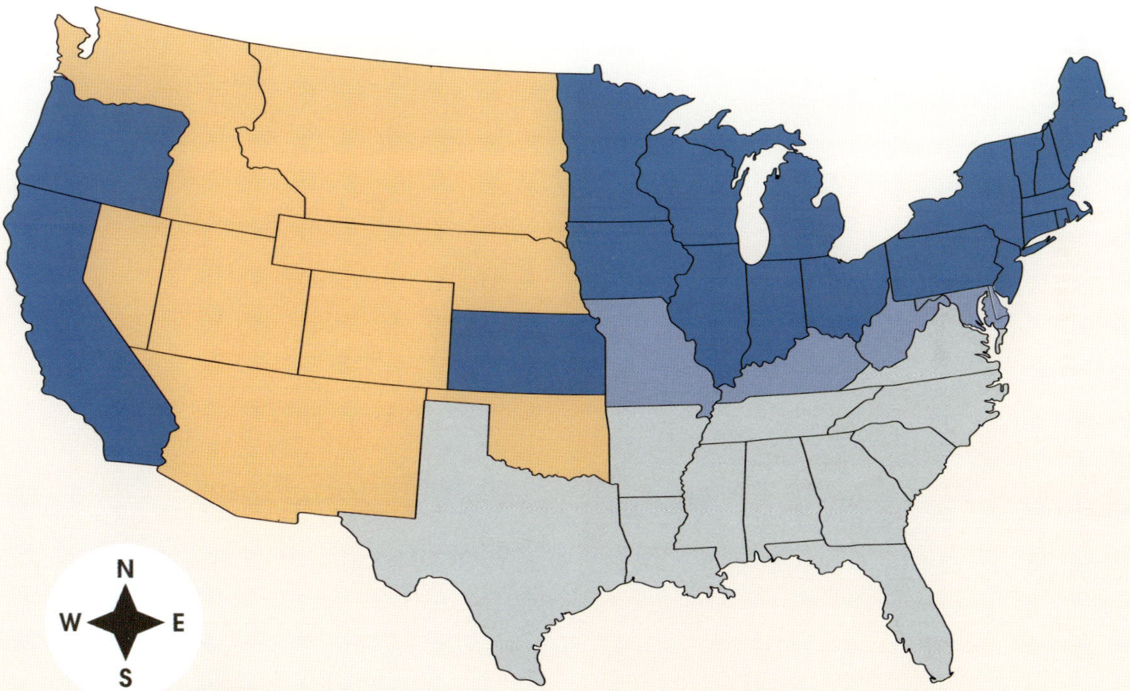

Union state

Union border state

Confederate state

Territory

IMPACTS OF THE PROCLAMATION

The Proclamation had many effects on the Civil War. It made it clear that the Union was against slavery. England and France had been secretly supporting the Confederacy. But these countries had abolished slavery themselves, so they could not publicly help the side fighting to keep it. Also, before the Proclamation, some white people in poverty in the South believed the war was about states' rights. This is the idea that states get to make decisions without the federal government getting involved. But the Proclamation made it clear that the war was about slavery. This turned these white southerners against rich enslavers, many of whom didn't have to fight in the war like they did.

The Proclamation freed no enslaved people in Delaware, Maryland, Kentucky, and Missouri. These four states were called the border states. They were on the boundary of the Confederacy. Slavery was still legal in these states. But the border states supported the Union.

When the Civil War started, President Lincoln had said that it was not about ending slavery in the South. It was about saving the Union. Lincoln believed

Abraham Lincoln was the sixteenth US president. In his writings and speeches, he frequently discussed the issue of slavery.

freeing enslaved people only in the states that had seceded would keep the border states from rebelling. Still, by signing the Emancipation Proclamation, Lincoln earned the nickname "the Great Emancipator."

GENERAL ORDER NO. 3

The Civil War ended in 1865. On April 9, Confederate general Robert E. Lee surrendered to Union general

Today, people can attend Juneteenth celebration services at Reedy Chapel A.M.E. Church, where a copy of General Order No. 3 is believed to have been posted.

Ulysses S. Grant in Appomattox Court House in Virginia. Historians estimate that by the end of the war, between 620,000 and 750,000 soldiers had died.

Once the war was over, the Union army needed to occupy former Confederate territories and inform everyone that enslaved people would now be free. It took two more months for Union soldiers to arrive in Galveston, Texas. Major General Gordon Granger was sent to Texas to establish order. When Granger arrived, he took over the largest building in town. That became his headquarters. There, Granger wrote General Order No. 3. At the nearby customs house, several copies of the Juneteenth Order, as it was sometimes

PERSPECTIVES

FIGURING OUT FREEDOM

Many enslaved people had different ideas about what freedom meant. Some formerly enslaved people were excited and left the plantations immediately. But others were unsure of what to do next. Felix Haywood was a formerly enslaved Black man in San Antonio, Texas. He said some people "seemed to want to get closer to freedom so they knew what it was—like it was a place or a city." He also said, "We knew freedom was on us, but we didn't know what was to come with it. We thought we were going to get rich. . . . We soon found out that freedom could make folks proud, but it didn't make them rich."

called, were printed. The order was then passed around the city.

Many Black people heard the news from their overseers and enslavers, who gathered the enslaved people on their plantations and read the order aloud. Other Black people heard the news from Union soldiers traveling around Texas. Some heard about it from other Black people who had seen notices posted at places such as the Negro Church on Broadway. However they heard the news, June 19 marked the date when the last enslaved people in the South officially learned of their freedom.

The nationwide end of slavery did not come until the Thirteenth Amendment was added to the US Constitution. It passed on December 6, 1865. It officially abolished slavery in the United States.

STRAIGHT TO THE SOURCE

General Order No. 3 was issued by Major General Gordon Granger. His name and the name of his assistant, Major Frederick Emery, appear on the order. General Order No. 3 states the following:

> *The people of Texas are informed that, in accordance with a proclamation from the Executive of the United States, all slaves are free. This involves an absolute equality of personal rights and rights of property between former masters and slaves, and the connection heretofore existing between them becomes that between employer and hired labor. The freedmen are advised to remain quietly at their present homes and work for wages. They are informed that they will not be allowed to collect at military posts and that they will not be supported in idleness either there or elsewhere.*

Source: Michael Davis. "National Archives Safeguards Original 'Juneteenth' General Order." *National Archives News*, 19 June 2020, archives.gov. Accessed 28 Apr. 2023.

CONSIDER YOUR AUDIENCE

Adapt this passage for a different audience, such as the readers of a newspaper. Write a newspaper article conveying this same information for the new audience. How does your article differ from the original text and why?

CHAPTER FOUR

JUNETEENTH CELEBRATIONS

Juneteenth was first celebrated in 1866 in Black communities around Texas. One celebration took place in Galveston at the same church where General Order No. 3 had been posted. Now known as Reedy Chapel, the church was the last stop on a march from the county courthouse. Churches were often the main sites of early Juneteenth celebrations. This was because prayer was very important to many formerly enslaved people. Black men, women, and children wore their

In 1900, a Juneteenth celebration took place at Wheeler's Grove, now known as Eastwoods Park, in Austin, Texas. The event featured a band, parade, and picnic, along with other activities.

finest clothes to these events. A much larger celebration occurred in Houston, Texas. It included a parade and a barbecue. Marshals on horseback directed thousands of Black people along the main street. This went so smoothly that celebrations continued every year. Over time, these celebrations began including more activities, such as baseball games and dance parties.

Juneteenth celebrations usually involved lots of food too. Many of these foods were red. This color is important in many West African cultures. Red symbolizes power, sacrifice, and transformation. Some popular foods were red beans and rice, punch, and strawberries. Barbecue meats were also popular, especially when covered with a rich red sauce. Juneteenth gave people an opportunity to cook together as a community.

During early Juneteenth celebrations, many people also focused on honoring elders. Elders shared their experiences during slavery. They taught younger generations about their history.

At modern Juneteenth celebrations, people often grill meats. Some events also feature food trucks owned by Black vendors.

JUNETEENTH AND CIVIL RIGHTS

Even though Black people were free after 1865, many still weren't treated as equals. Throughout the South, lawmakers passed new laws called black codes. One code prevented formerly enslaved people from gathering in public places. But Black people still found ways to celebrate. In 1872, four Black men in Houston raised money to buy land on which they could celebrate Juneteenth. They named the area Emancipation Park.

Black people found other ways to celebrate privately. They held picnics at churches and had backyard barbecues. They would not stop celebrating

Throughout the 1950s and 1960s, many people fought to win equal rights for Black people. In August 1963, thousands participated in the March on Washington for Jobs and Freedom in Washington, DC.

their freedom. Throughout the 1900s, millions of Black people moved out of the South, bringing their celebrations to other parts of the country.

There weren't many large Juneteenth celebrations in the early 1900s. It was not yet a federal holiday, so people were not given time off work or school to celebrate. Black people also faced discrimination. Many did not have the right to vote. Some Southern states even passed laws to make voting more difficult for Black people. Black people also faced segregation, the practice of separating people according to race.

Black and white people in the South were not allowed to attend the same schools, shop in the same stores, or eat at the same places.

But during the civil rights movement of the 1950s and 1960s, Juneteenth took on a new meaning. At this time, Black people were fighting for equality. They battled for equal voting rights and resisted segregation. Civil rights leaders connected their struggle to the struggle of their enslaved ancestors. Through activism and nonviolent protest, many people

PERSPECTIVES

JUNETEENTH MEMORIES

Annette Gordon-Reed is a professor of history and law at Harvard University. She was born in Texas and grew up celebrating Juneteenth. For Gordon-Reed, Juneteenth is a celebration of the freedom her ancestors and relatives had known. She said, "Although there was a very long way to go before we had full and equal citizenship, we were able to gather together as a family to celebrate." It was also a summer holiday. Gordon-Reed remembers "playing games, throwing firecrackers, and lighting sparklers until night fell."

In 2021, 94-year-old Opal Lee, *second from left*, was invited to watch President Joe Biden, *center*, sign the bill making Juneteenth a federal holiday. Lee is often called the Grandmother of Juneteenth.

worked to end inequality. In 1964, President Lyndon B. Johnson signed the Civil Rights Act. This law made segregation illegal. That same year, the Twenty-Fourth Amendment was passed. It outlawed discriminatory voting practices, making voting easier for Black people. Juneteenth became an opportunity to celebrate victories in the civil rights movement. More people began celebrating the holiday again.

JUNETEENTH TODAY

In 1980, Texas became the first state to make Juneteenth a state holiday. Soon after, several other states started recognizing the holiday. Through the efforts of people like civil rights activist Opal Lee, Juneteenth became nationally known. On June 17, 2021, President Joe Biden signed a bill into law making Juneteenth a federal holiday.

Today, Juneteenth celebrations are commemorated much like early ones. They feature parades, barbecues, fireworks, and musical performances. Cities across the country plan celebrations featuring Black artists and musicians.

SOCIAL JUSTICE

Many Juneteenth celebrations focus on social justice activism. Social justice activists work to make things fair for people across all communities. Some people may be treated unfairly because of racism. They may have different opportunities because of the color of their skin. They may not be able to get the same jobs or live in the same places. Sometimes they may even be told to wear their hair differently. Social justice activists raise awareness about issues that Black Americans face. They march, protest, and ask politicians to change laws. Some people even run for political office so they can make new laws.

Juneteenth celebrations often feature musicians and dance performances. Many of these performances celebrate Black American culture and African heritage.

At Emancipation Park in Texas, local Black creators sell their goods. People participate in a run to raise money for the park. In many cities around the country, people also march and protest. They connect the historical struggles of enslaved Black people with the unfair treatment many people of color still face today. Just like civil rights leaders, they see Juneteenth as a time to participate in peaceful activism and work toward change.

Juneteenth continues to be an important holiday for many people in the United States. It gives people a chance to remember their history, honor their ancestors, and participate in the fight to end inequality. It is a time for people to celebrate freedom, remembering the past while fighting for the future.

FURTHER EVIDENCE

Chapter Four discusses Juneteenth celebrations. What was the main point of this chapter? What evidence is included to support this point? Read the article at the website below. Does the information on the website support the main point of the chapter? Does it present new evidence?

CELEBRATING JUNETEENTH

abdocorelibrary.com/juneteenth

IMPORTANT DATES

Late 1400s–1500s CE
The transatlantic slave trade begins.

1619
Enslaved Black people arrive in Jamestown, Virginia.

1860
Abraham Lincoln is elected president. South Carolina becomes the first state to secede from the Union.

1861
The American Civil War begins.

1863
President Lincoln signs the Emancipation Proclamation.

1865
The Civil War ends in April. General Order No. 3 is posted two months later, on June 19. The Thirteenth Amendment passes.

1866
The first Juneteenth celebration is held in Galveston, Texas.

1964
The Civil Rights Act is signed into law. The Twenty-Fourth Amendment is added to the Constitution.

1980
Texas recognizes Juneteenth as an official state holiday.

2021
President Joe Biden signs a bill making Juneteenth a federal holiday.

STOP AND THINK

Why Do I Care?

Maybe you have never celebrated Juneteenth before. But that doesn't mean you can't think about why it is an important holiday. Why is it important to remember the past and learn more about Black American history? Are there any Juneteenth celebrations or events in your state?

Surprise Me

Chapter One discusses a modern Juneteenth celebration. After reading this book, what two or three facts about Juneteenth celebrations did you find most surprising? Write a few sentences about each fact. Why did you find each fact surprising?

Take a Stand

Chapter Four discusses Juneteenth's focus on equality, civil rights, and social justice. Why do you think it is important to focus on these things on Juneteenth? Do you think all people can benefit from celebrating Juneteenth and learning about the history of slavery in the United States?

Dig Deeper

After reading this book, what questions do you still have about Juneteenth? With an adult's help, find a few reliable sources that can help you answer your questions. Write a paragraph about what you learned.

GLOSSARY

abolitionist
a person who opposes the practice of slavery and works to end it

activism
a practice that encourages strong action to bring about change

amendment
a change or addition

anniversary
the date on which an event took place in an earlier year

economy
the system of how money is made in a region

justify
to prove that something is right or reasonable

race
the social idea that people can be divided into groups based on physical characteristics such as skin color

rebellion
a fight against a government or ruler

sacrifice
to give up something of great value for a belief or to show loyalty

surrender
to yield to the control of another group or person

ONLINE RESOURCES

To learn more about Juneteenth, visit our free resource websites below.

Core Library CONNECTION
FREE! COMMON CORE MULTIMEDIA RESOURCES

Visit **abdocorelibrary.com** or scan this QR code for free Common Core resources for teachers and students, including vetted activities, multimedia, and booklinks, for deeper subject comprehension.

Booklinks NONFICTION NETWORK
FREE! ONLINE NONFICTION RESOURCES

Visit **abdobooklinks.com** or scan this QR code for free additional online weblinks for further learning. These links are routinely monitored and updated to provide the most current information available.

LEARN MORE

Gale, Ryan. *Fact and Fiction of the Civil War.* Abdo, 2022.

Jewel, Kirsti. *What Is Juneteenth?* Penguin Workshop, 2022.

Sjonger, Rebecca. *Frederick Douglass.* Crabtree, 2021.

INDEX

About the Author

Shasta Clinch is a freelance copy editor and proofreader. She lives with her husband and two lovely littles in New Jersey.